SCHOENBERG

Oxford Studies of Composers

Oxford Studies of Composers (5)

SCHOENBERG

ANTHONY PAYNE

London
OXFORD UNIVERSITY PRESS
NEW YORK TORONTO

Oxford University Press, Ely House, London W. 1

GLASGOW   NEW YORK   TORONTO   MELBOURNE   WELLINGTON
CAPE TOWN   IBADAN   NAIROBI   DAR ES SALAAM   LUSAKA   ADDIS ABABA
DELHI   BOMBAY   CALCUTTA   MADRAS   KARACHI   LAHORE   DACCA
KUALA LUMPUR   SINGAPORE   HONG KONG   TOKYO

ISBN 0 19 314116 7

© Oxford University Press 1968

First published 1968
Reprinted 1969, 1972, *and* 1974

ACKNOWLEDGEMENTS

Grateful acknowledgements are due to the following for permission to
quote from the works named: Universal Edition (London) Ltd., and
Belmont Music Publishers, Los Angeles (the Chamber Symphony, the
Second and Third String Quartets, *Das Buch der hängenden Gärten, Pierrot
Lunaire, Erwartung*, Suite Op. 29, and Variations for Orchestra), Hinrichsen
Edition Ltd., London, the copyright holders of Peters Edition (Five
Orchestral Pieces), Mr. Lawrence Schoenberg, Belmont Music Publishers,
Los Angeles (*Die Jakobsleiter*), G. Schirmer Inc., New York (the Violin and
Piano Concertos, and the Fourth String Quartet), Wilhelm Hansen,
Copenhagen (Five Piano Pieces, copyright 1923–51), Bote & Bock, Berlin
(Six Pieces for Male Chorus, by permission of the original publishers Bote
& Bock Berlin/Wiesbaden, © 1930, 1958, by Bote & Bock Berlin), and
Boelke-Bomart, Inc. (the String Trio, Op. 45).

PRINTED IN GREAT BRITAIN
This impression printed by photolithography from the
original printing by W & J Mackay Limited, Chatham

PREFACE

I T would have been impossible, in what amounts to an extended essay, to deal in depth with every item of such a varied output as Schoenberg's. An examination of one aspect of the composer's work was obviously called for, and it seemed that style and form as these grew out of his psychological and expressive needs gave the best opportunities for probing beneath the music's surface. In this way one could direct attention beyond the historical significance of the composer's linguistic discoveries, a factor which has too often been allowed to overshadow the artistic content of the music itself. The choice of works for discussion has been dictated solely by the needs of this subject, and consequently some of the composer's greatest works have been ignored, among them, regrettably, all but one of the operas. All critical methods which are not directly concerned with an understanding of the music of individual works have been avoided. Thus comparative evaluations are not to be found, for to say that the rhythmic procedures of the twelve-note works are less enterprising than those of, say, *Erwartung* or to find a more successful avoidance of tonality in the Five Orchestral Pieces than in the First Chamber Symphony is to begin to forget that each work is a law unto itself, attempting to symbolize a unique expressive concept, and is not merely a further stage in the composer's stylistic development.

CONTENTS

LIST OF SCHOENBERG'S PRINCIPAL WORKS
IN CHRONOLOGICAL ORDER

String Sextet: Verklärte Nacht, opus 4—1899
Gurrelieder—1900-11
Pelleas und Melisande, Symphonic Poem, opus 5—1903
First String Quartet, opus 7—1905
First Chamber Symphony, opus 9—1906
Second String Quartet, opus 10—1908
Three Piano Pieces, opus 11—1909
Das Buch der hängenden Gärten, opus 15—1909
Five Orchestral Pieces, opus 16—1909
Erwartung, Monodrama, opus 17—1909
Pierrot Lunaire, opus 21—1912
Die Glückliche Hand, Drama with music, opus 18—1913
Die Jakobsleiter, Oratorio (unfinished)—1917
Five Piano Pieces, opus 23—1920-3
Serenade, opus 24—1923
Suite for Piano, opus 25—1921-3
Wind Quintet, opus 26—1924
Suite, opus 29—1925
Third String Quartet, opus 30—1927
Variations for Orchestra, opus 31—1926-8
Von Heute auf Morgen, Opera in one act, opus 32—1929
Six Pieces for Male Chorus, opus 35—1930
Moses und Aron, Opera in three acts (unfinished)—1930-2
Suite in G for String Orchestra—1934
Violin Concerto, opus 36—1934-6
Fourth String Quartet, opus 37—1936
Second Chamber Symphony, opus 38—1906-39
Ode to Napoleon Buonaparte, opus 41—1942
Piano Concerto, opus 42—1942
String Trio, opus 45—1946
A Survivor from Warsaw, opus 46—1947
Phantasy for Violin, with piano accompaniment, opus 47—1949

THE BACKGROUND

The spiritual and psychological reasons for Schoenberg's revolutionary musical procedures are of crucial importance to an understanding of his art, and an assessment of what was at stake in his inner world should complement an exposition of the extraordinary ways and means by which he renewed musical language and feeling at the beginning of this century. The twelve-note method with which he found an answer to his compositional problems in mid-career was by no means the inevitable outcome of late-Romantic chromaticism. Other composers, Scriabin, Debussy, and Strauss among them, had brought music to a state analogous to that of Schoenberg's at the turn of the century, yet they had sought different answers in accordance with their temperamental needs, or else, like Strauss, had drawn back from the threshold which Schoenberg strode over. In fact, the liberating influence which twelve-note serialism was to become to so many diverse creative natures can be said to have originated in the psychological needs of one man. It was only one of several possible solutions to twentieth-century problems, as seems to be confirmed by the subsequent development of largely unrelated techniques.

The musical situation which faced Schoenberg at the beginning of his career was dominated by the motivic power of Brahms, and by the all-pervading harmonic influence of *Tristan* and *Parsifal*. These were factors impossible to ignore for a composer who felt himself to belong to the Austro-German tradition. Before *Tristan*, tonality, the bastion of post-Renaissance form, had been chiefly established by cadence. The full cadential statement phrased musical paragraphs and orientated them, while its postponement by various means promoted argument and development. In *Tristan*, Wagner undermined this system by continual avoidance of the positive cadence which would have clinched a key. He extended and varied the process by a wholesale use of ambiguous chromatic chords, chords which previous composers had employed merely to colour their harmony or to modulate. The 'Tristan-chord', for instance, can behave in a variety of ways, each hinting through enharmonic logic at new key areas which are themselves rarely established (Ex. 1). One could call this a technique of endless modulation or allusion to key areas without positive statement, and yet by the end of the opera we have come to accept the progression 1a as a satisfying entity in itself. This establishes one of the most important principles of

Ex. 1a Langsam

Ex. 1b Immer sehr ruhig

Ex. 1c Sehr lebhaft

construction in atonal forms: the use of referential features as a substitute for the orientation to be gained from tonality. The 'Tristan' progression and similar elements, although unstably chromatic by the laws of tonality, come to perform the duties of positive cadence, even if Wagner, keeping as near as he does to tonality, can ease tension with an orthodox resolution in the final bars.

A further feature to which Schoenberg found himself heir, as did Strauss, Wolf, and Mahler, was an increasing melodic angularity stemming from moments of agony in *Tristan* and *Parsifal*, where lines leapt and twisted in response to the anguish of the dramatic situation, frequently avoiding contact with the notes of the underlying harmony in an additional bid for acute expressive tension (Ex. 2). To these factors, the disruptive melodic lines, avoidance of positive cadence and tonal ambiguity of chromatic chords, can be added another of crucial importance. The logical step from music which, like *Tristan*'s, transforms

Ex. 2 Impetuoso

chords of the seventh into referential features comparable to cadential triads, is to a music where tonality begins to disappear completely. Harmonies will exist in themselves rather than for the logic of key, and the chord structures of thirds and fifths required by tonal practice will cease to be necessary. As a result of this development several composers at the turn of the century started to build chords synthetically out of fourths and whole-tone intervals, or, like Scriabin, constructed complex aggregations of intervals for which tonality had no precedent (Ex. 3).

Ex. 3

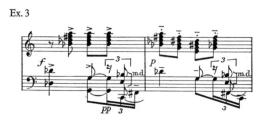

THE EARLY PERIOD

All these elements are to be seen variously deployed throughout Schoenberg's first creative period, appearing at their most highly developed in the First Chamber Symphony, an achievement which represents the culmination of his early style. It is a work which still depends to some extent on tonality for its formal articulation, and accordingly its single movement is laid out in expanded sonata form. But there is an increasingly equivocal relationship between harmony and melody, which would generate a motion considerably different from the norm of classical and romantic structures, if it were not for the still conventional rhythmic forms. These give the work its thrust, and help us to orientate ourselves structurally when the harmonic quicksands shift uneasily beneath our feet. At the same time, the loosening of tonal bonds within the work places an added burden on melodic writing as a means of articulating form, and this emphasizes the use of pure counterpoint—a factor which will be of paramount importance in later works which abandon tonality completely. Formally the work's sonata structure is combined with the elements of a four-movement symphony, and is laid out in the pattern Exposition–Scherzo–Development–Slow movement–Recapitulation cum Finale. The first significant fact to arise from this ground plan is the lack of space for traditional development—in contrast to the earlier First String Quartet, another four-in-one structure, which had made room for two large working-out sections. The traditional development section was dependent on a firm progress through strongly defined key areas, and the attendant growth and interaction of themes was pointed by a flow of harmony which was dictated from the bass line, and which, if apparently contrapuntal, was only so in terms of harmonic elaboration. Such procedures were becoming incompatible both with the growing importance of polyphony in Schoenberg's style, and with the ambiguous harmonies which necessitated that polyphony and which in turn were fed by it. As a result, the Chamber Symphony's development section differs little from other sections which also progress by continual polyphonic elaboration and so exemplify already the technique of constantly varied repetition typical of the composer's maturity. This polyphony frequently flows for long stretches without really suggesting key (Ex. 5) and the fact that many such paragraphs end in tonal cadence should not lead us to overemphasize the structural importance of tonality. The absence of key-feeling prior to these terminal points sometimes lends them an arbitrary air, and in theory their punctuating function could be replaced by one of many referential features, harmonic, melodic, or rhythmic. This fact is emphasized by the cadential use of fourth chords between the slow movement and development, where they appear without any hint of key.

Granted that free polyphony was becoming the chief agent of form-building in place of tonality, there remained the problem of how to order this kind of texture vertically. For hundreds of years this dimension had been governed by tonality; that is to say it had been anchored to a strongly harmonic bass and confined to third-dominated harmony. Even in the previous age of modal polyphony, where the dynamism resulting from key journeys was missing, the vertical aspect of linear writing had been ordered by a strictly limiting triadic law. The sense of harmonic progression in the Baroque and after, which permitted more dissonant contrapuntal complexes, becomes increasingly obscured in early Schoenberg, and this places his freer counterpoint on a par with pre-Baroque procedures. Yet his synthetic chord building and repudiation of the boundary between consonance and dissonance present no points of contact with the harmonic aspects of Renaissance polyphony. Ultimately, the interaction of vertical and horizontal in the Chamber Symphony is by no means fully systematized, and depends on various procedures which operate irrationally in a way that later Schoenberg would not countenance. It took a work like the Five Orchestral Pieces to solve more radically the problems posed by the loosening of tonality, but in the present work a tonal residue remains, and the attempt to essay a large-scale form with tonal elements as well as paragraphs and ideas which lack key yields a specialized and not always satisfactory answer to stylistic questions which did not recur.

The melodic flowering which marks part of the first section's main subject is typical of the half-way house achieved by Schoenberg at this time. Initially the harmonic background appears tonal (Ex. 4); setting

Ex. 4

out with a strong feeling of E as dominant, enhanced by the traditional augmented sixth in the fourth bar and a Neapolitan inflexion two bars later, it moves through unambiguous tonal areas to F minor. Yet in its bid to saturate the texture with chromaticism, the polyphony is so rich in decorated passing notes, appoggiaturas, and suspensions that the ear is hard put in performance to trace the tonal logic, especially if the composer's fast metronome marking is adhered to. The melodies seem on the point of complete linear independence, and the harmonies which underpin them begin to sound like a method for tying together the lines step by step, instead of a progression in its own right with forward-moving structural properties. The incorporation of such writing into a dynamic sonata movement is justified more by the energy-giving properties of the traditional phrase-lengths and rhythms than by its stylistically more advanced aspects. Other passages possess far less tonal justification, and realize more radically and, it would appear, truthfully, the sound concept which Ex. 4 shies away from. The development contains a concentration of this kind of writing, where for a time the combination of melodic strands is ruled by a far wider concept of tonality (Ex. 5) than in Ex. 4. The three-part canon which forms the

Ex. 5

Sehr rasch

burden of this passage uses a theme which has fairly strong if wide-ranging tonal implications—it has been simply harmonized on two previous occasions with unrelated triads—but when it is worked in counterpoint the tonal polarities begin to merge and blur. The initial entries on F, C, and A lose significance, as does the D minor chord which punctuated the previous section, although such features do show that even the most advanced of the composer's procedures set out from tonal premises. Something of this manner of thought is also to be seen in the way certain canonic features do not imitate exactly (*a* in Ex. 5). The explanation for this seems to be that the resultant vertical coincidences provided for Schoenberg a vague echo of the tonality (albeit of a Wagnerian complexity) which he was soon to deny himself completely.

If the lines here have been given their head and then adjusted

Ex. 6

somewhat arbitrarily, a more systematic limitation of the vertical possibilities occasioned by highly chromatic counterpoint is found in a subsequent passage (Ex. 6). Here the whole-tone construction of the dominating theme (*x*) is expanded to embrace the entire texture, and dictates the placing of the scherzo theme (*y*) whose entries on A flat and G flat put the total thematic complex within the bounds of the whole-tone scale on C. The semitonal kink in the highest voice at the end of the first bar merely refers back to the theme's original shape in the scherzo section, and it can be seen how the phrase is then manipulated in order to continue within the same whole-tone scale—the answering part brings the features totally within the scale. Even alien elements like the transition theme (*z*) find prominent notes conforming with the whole-tone complex, and this tendency becomes more prevalent as the section drives to its climax. At this point the whole texture breaks into streams of augmented triads moving in contrary motion, across which is thrown the leading motive in fourths. The movement of parts is so organized that any cross-section through the score will give notes belonging to a single whole-tone scale (the overlapping of the statements in fourths provides a single exception which accentuates the phrase-lengths). We feel here that a dynamic climax has been reached, and the increasing dominance of the fourths motive into which the total sound subsequently resolves provides, as was suggested above, a point of reference which neatly cadences without tonal commitment. The lack of an audibly defined tonality at nearly every stage, however, has been a denial of the sort of dynamic progress achieved by earlier sonata developments. A sense of purpose has been maintained by driving rhythms and by the increasing melodic complexity and harmonic density of the counterpoint. In Ex. 5, for instance, the meandering effect of the contrapuntal strands is counterbalanced by the melodic growth in the top part, whose phrase-lengths become longer and more rhythmically active. But this intense activity takes place against a static harmonic background, since the tensions inherent in the rapidly modulating and frequently ambiguous harmonic allusions cancel themselves into immobility. This subtle interplay between static and dynamic elements in harmony, melody, and rhythm becomes one of the most fascinating aspects of Schoenberg's fully atonal period.

Perhaps some of the tonal practices in the Chamber Symphony are more apparent to the eye than to the ear—as in, say, the vertical ordering of textures whose polyphonic sense moves beyond key—but Schoenberg still seemed in his own mind to be working outwards from tonal points of reference. His next important work, however, the Second String Quartet, takes steps to sever tonal bonds completely, and the fact that parts of it are as overtly tonal as anything in the Chamber Symphony makes it one of the most fascinating of all transitional works, unsatisfactory from the point of view of stylistic unity, perhaps, and a little unsure of its course and ultimate destination in the uncharted seas of atonality, but, for that very reason, a work of heroic exploration. Here one can see Schoenberg's early attempts to articulate sentences and paragraphs in the absence of tonality, and to construct larger forms appropriate to the new keyless material. The Chamber Symphony had still managed to utilize classical ideas of form in, for example, its contrasted subject groups, its feeling for cumulative sonata development, and in such traditional processes as the heightened expectancy at the close of the exposition—even if a certain tonal ambiguity in melody and harmony placed increasing weight on rhythm in achieving this compromise. But the Second Quartet begins a search for new forms which was to occupy the composer for the next seven or eight years, and yielded a plethora of solutions, each seemingly a unique answer to unique expressive problems. As much could be said of any classical masterpiece, but there is a difference between the continual rethinking of form in Schoenberg and the structural processes of his predecessors, who composed against a background of traditionally viable patterns.

The last two movements of the quartet introduce a soprano part in settings of words by Stefan George. This is significant, since an all-important prop to musical construction in nearly all extended forms throughout Schoenberg's 'free' atonal period was the sense of logical continuity and varied pace to be gained from words. Significant also is the use in the third movement of variations, perhaps the most suscept-ible of all classical forms to the freely associative fantasy typical of atonality, and a natural embodiment of the continuously varied restate-ment which had obsessed the composer even before his abandonment of key. This movement is, in fact, notated in the key of E flat minor, but such references as there are to the key are merely used to limit the pitches at which certain material can be stated, and this tonal element is only one among several of a melodic and rhythmic nature in a movement which deals in referential features rather than tonality. The finale actually does away with a key signature altogether, and there is a more obvious attempt here to keep all twelve notes of the chromatic scale continually before the listener (Ex. 7), but the difference between the

Ex. 7

two movements is more in the attitude of the composer to his material than in anything that we can hear.

A glance at the theme on which the third movement's variations are built (Ex. 8a) and at one of the variations itself (Ex. 8b) will show the literally all-pervading motive work—one method at least of giving every facet of the texture a *raison d'être* in the absence of tonal movement, and a point which is characteristic of other atonal composers, as can be seen, for instance, in Webern's pre-twelve-note works. Ex. 8b also spotlights the increased importance of contrapuntal thought, for, as was suggested earlier, the absence of the sense supplied by tonal harmonic movement places more weight on horizontal line and on its chief means of articula-tion, interval and rhythm. But if motive working justifies the presence of nearly every figure in a movement like the Second Quartet's theme and variations, it cannot dictate the placing of those figures in time and space, in other words their horizontal succession and vertical ordering. Not until the advent of serialism did this crucial aspect of musical form begin to be

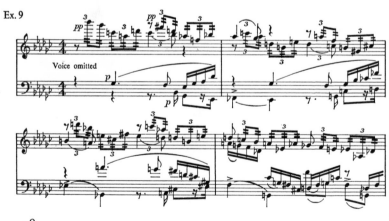

systematized, and we may now look at several works written prior to this formulation to sample some of Schoenberg's solutions to the problem of deploying and developing atonal themes in a broad formal context.

Taking a passage like Ex. 9 from the Second Quartet, we can say that as far as the immediate spacing of material is concerned (to ignore for the moment the problem of stringing out ideas at length) the chromaticism which contributes to the increasing atonality is itself a result of the heightened dependence on melody and counterpoint. For the refusal of

Ex. 9

the thematic ideas in this example to share notes in common, or to coalesce into harmonies which would bind them into a suave vertical unity, is dictated by the intention to give individuality to each part, a procedure which contributes much to the concept of keeping all twelve notes in play. At the same time there are moments like Ex. 10 from the

Ex. 10

scherzo, where the lack of strict imitation indicates an ear that still builds harmonies tonally, even if their sequence belies their structure. Here the line is doubled with major and minor thirds rather than an exact parallel line. This reinforces harmony and suggests a lingering unwillingness to accept the full implication of the widely ranging melody.

The problem of an order of events in such a movement is also an acute one, and in the Quartet, apart from the first movement, where the style is still tonal enough to admit some sort of sonata form, one can see Schoenberg putting together movements out of shorter sequences. It is as if the concentrated motivic and contrapuntal working needed to produce a fairly short paragraph carries the weight of a much larger tonal equivalent. Hence the concentrated burst of each of the variations, which, linked together, form that movement, and, again, the short sections which are juxtaposed in the scherzo. In fact, one can say that one of Schoenberg's main problems, as a naturally expansive artist, was to see how a large form was both technically and, more important, aesthetically possible when his increasing polyphonic elaboration and formal compression were continually reducing the ratio of time to density of experience: how, in fact, to place the short pregnant phrases of his free atonal style in a new context, divorced from the extreme emotional pressure which had necessitated their development from late-Romanticism.

THE FIVE ORCHESTRAL PIECES

Schoenberg's first compositions came at the end of an era much of whose art had relied primarily on a personal response to life. In the hands of Debussy this led to Impressionism, which lived at the nerve ends, while in Mahler, Schoenberg and briefly in Strauss, a further logical extension ended in a full-scale plunge into the subconscious. The half-lit dreams, phantasmagoria, imaginary fears and tensions of this demi-world erupted into suitably tortured harmonies, melodic lines, and forms. Nevertheless, as can be seen from the verses which are set in the Second Quartet, such inner exploration provides the seed of self-knowledge which in a courageous soul can lead to self-denial and spiritual victory. Paradoxically, it was through Expressionism, as the new style was termed, that Schoenberg eventually discovered twelve-note writing. For the twelve-note method gave him the detachment he needed to construct larger forms out of the Expressionist fragments.

For the time being, however, Schoenberg was grappling with the formal problems posed by the new style. The Five Orchestral Pieces give us a compendium of the methods he used to limit the infinity of possibilities suggested by the abandonment of tonality, or, one might say, to choose from the almost frightening new range of feelings which had become accessible with his new awareness of the subconscious. It has already been suggested that movements grew shorter at this time owing to the increasing complexity of texture which packs musical experience into shorter time spans, but it would be evading an important issue merely to ascribe this complexity to the high-pressure demands of Expressionism, or, compositionally, to the need for all-pervasive motive work to govern textures in the absence of tonality.

The length of a classical sonata exposition, varying from half to about a third of the length of the movement, was dictated by the need to establish the tonic and the move to the dominant. This primary factor made it possible to set out thematic material in a leisurely way; indeed, it sometimes necessitated the employment of ideas which would not be of much use later, merely to fill out the length needed to give a balanced statement of the tonic-dominant relationships. Atonal forms make no such demands upon the composer, since all that now needs to be exposed is the material. Consequently, this section is invariably short, and development begins almost immediately. Again, recapitulation in the classical sense is not necessary, for there is no longer a need to complete designs with a celebration of the home key and the attendant repetition of themes. This is a further reason for the continual variation practised by Schoenberg.

The first of the Five Orchestral Pieces is just such a piece. Only a fifth of its length is utilized for the purposes of exposition, and the rest is taken up with a development of ideas which is worth detailed examination.

Ex. 11

The exposition, shown complete in Ex. 11, is itself a mine of information, presenting ideas in an apparently spasmodic fashion, but evolving themes steadily and already establishing links between every facet of the texture. Later, an increasingly close juxtaposition of themes, which also develop in shape, reveals an intricate network of further interrelationships. The first three bars already present three ideas of importance: (1) the semiquaver bass with its prominent cell of a semitone followed by an augmented fourth (*a*), a perfect fourth (*b*), or a major third (*c*); (2) the middle part whose open fifths and rhythm, shared with the top line, are germinal; (3) the top line itself, whose accentuated notes pick out an all-important augmented triad, F–A–C sharp, and which sets out by inverting (*c*), then repeating it sequentially. The opening sentence is completed by an even shorter phrase: (*c*) inverted grows a chromatic head, expands (*a*) to span an octave and then diminishes its rhythm (bar 6 provides a punctuation mark). The next phrase (*x*) starts out in an apparently new direction, but it can be related several times over to the opening. It is a rhythmic expansion of the top line, feels like an inversion of it with changed intervals, also incorporates a retrograde inversion of (*c*), and grows a tail-piece (*y*). The following three-bar figure only appears once later on—perhaps in composing quickly Schoenberg thought that such a figure would be of subsequent use only to find the possibilities in his other material rich enough for his purposes. The five bars beginning at 15, however, are of the utmost importance. The first segment of (*z*) juggles notes from the bass in the first bar, then tops this with (*y*). Meanwhile (*x*), above, shows a closer relationship to (*c*), and then develops its tail by rhythmic augmentation and by inversion, suggesting yet another afterthought (*d*), which, again, is a retrograde relation to the opening top line. The section ends with another statement of the punctuation mark. At the same time, the augmented (*y*) changes its shape to reveal a resemblance to further previous details, and then launches the final downward swoop, itself a summary of earlier features.

Such motivic density is characteristic of nearly all Schoenberg's work at this period, and indeed, throughout his life. 'Nacht', from *Pierrot lunaire*, for instance, shows a texture completely saturated with a single motive cell E–G–E flat and its transpositions. In this instance motivic work has not yet controlled the actual pitch at which material is stated. But in other movements it does, and so diverse are Schoenberg's methods at this time that one has to search each piece anew for a principle to govern its peculiar procedures. But it has been said with justice that none of Schoenberg's compositional methods before twelve-note writing consistently limits the possibilities of harmonic or thematic working to the point of yielding predictable results such as one finds in that method. We should not apply to this period analytical methods suitable for works based on pre-compositionally determined factors. Analysis can discover systematic elements in much of the writing after the event, but more elusive factors were frequently at work during the act of composition. In the exposition just described, for instance, we must admit that much is governed by free association, despite the elaborate network of motives, and by the fact that the composer seems to have heard the note D as a tonic, or, perhaps more accurately, as a point of reference. (Why else should (x) be stated at the pitch it is, or As, B flats, and C sharps—quasi-dominant features—provide points of orientation?) Later on, although by no means exclusively, Schoenberg seems also to have been swayed by the desire to avoid octave doublings.

Though Schoenberg cogently related the shape of the various links in the opening chain, the stages of the thematic process have of necessity been loosely strung out to facilitate clear exposition. There has been comparatively little overlap in these stages, and no sense of rhythmic purpose. The aim of the rest of the movement is to weave the material into an ever-tightening contrapuntal web, perhaps the most obvious substitute for a tonally controlled form. Immediately after the end of Ex. 11 a vigorous ostinato sets in on the cellos, compounded from intervals with which the previous section has familiarized us. Settling down on an inversion of (x), it sets the music in motion. Superimpositions of this ostinato, in up to four parts at the climax, including augmented and doubly augmented note values, are followed by a four-part canon at intervals of one beat. This gives a background, steadily growing in complexity, over which can be heard an increasing engagement of thematic forces, a process which is clearly seen in the three presentations of the opening theme. These are separated by other thematic combinations which similarly grow and interact. The punctuating figure follows the first statement, crowds in on the second before this, replete with new growth, can be completed, and finally in its urgency anticipates the third. Also, the statement appears in increasingly close canon, and shows variations of shape within the familiar rhythmic pattern while retaining the accompanying fifths. Two more small examples must suffice to show the free association between some consecutive incidents in the score which enables Schoenberg to develop his musical thought with lightning speed. Immediately after the passage just discussed there is an apparently new thought which, in fact, combines a segment of the ostinato (related to (x), and through it to the opening) with the opening's bare fifths (Ex. 12). Then there is the haunting tick of Ex. 13, where a final statement of (*x*) supplies witn its last two notes the slightest hint for the piled-up chords which follow. (It is also worth noting that the last two chords in the upper stave of Ex. 13 closely resemble the crotchet chord in bar 3 of Ex. 11, and the whole passage shows clearly the interaction of melodic and harmonic entities.)

The steady increase in activity throughout the piece, the growing density of counterpoint, the revelation of new relationships, and the closer and closer juxtaposition of fragments all bear a strong resemblance to the new adjacencies obtainable in traditional polyphonic forms. One should be cautious of accepting rules for the vertical organization of the score too easily. But some harmonic equivalent, however tentative, must be discovered to match the tight melodic organization, if we are to illuminate Schoenberg's contrapuntal method.

Plainly one of the prime factors is the desire to avoid octaves. This performs an expressive function in producing denser harmonic textures and thus greater tension, and is also important in the articulation it gives to individual counterpoints. The sounding of an octave by two polyphonic strands obviously tends to tie them together, and in so doing accentuates, however briefly, a vertical relationship when forms increasingly require horizontal priority. A comparison of the first entries of the ostinato will show that the only divergences from the original patterns of notes in the second entry are engineered to avoid octaves with the other part. As a corollary, the traditional chord structures, based on thirds, which governed even some of the more advanced writing in the Second Quartet, also tend to lessen the horizontal character of melodies by vertical fusion, and the Five Orchestral Pieces show generally more pungency in the vertical clashes produced by the counterpoint.

Although the factors which limit such vertical arrangements must be sought anew in each movement, the composer's own rapidly developing, but always strongly characteristic harmonic palette obviously plays a big part. The liking for chords founded on fourths or fifths and tritones, for instance, colours a great deal of the writing. The opening three bars of Ex. 11 provide a typical instance of the kind of features to be found in Schoenberg's harmonic writing at this time. There is firstly a slight, but nevertheless crucial reference to D as a substitute tonic, then the harmonic preference mentioned above which yields E flat—B flat—A in the second bar (also, a straight descent of the part in fifths would have produced an F major triad—too overt a tonal reference). Next there is the whole-tone melodic motive of the upper line which dictates the second chord of the second bar, thus also avoiding a triad (E major). Finally there is the last chord, which relies on three factors: the tonic D, the typical tritone D–G sharp in conjunction with the fourth G sharp–C sharp, and the fifth D–A. (The notes A–G sharp–C sharp can also be justified motivically as being a conflation of the last three melodic notes of the top line.)

A little later in the movement the tonic D becomes of fundamental importance in forming the basis of a chord D–F sharp–C sharp, which acts as a continuous pedal for the rest of the piece. This spotlights a characteristic of Schoenberg's free atonal writing which is crucial to a deeper understanding of his art. For this unchanging background chord only confirms what we feel about this work as a whole, namely, that the abandonment of classical tonality has plunged music into an essentially static world. Gone is the logic of progression through outlying key areas and back to an original tonic, which had given a sense of forward motion to the music of the Baroque, Classical, and Romantic eras. The apparent motivic drive of some figures is an illusion, since the texture as a whole is no longer governed by a system of dissonance and consonance whereby chords are resolved and thus keys stated. In a sense, music has turned full circle to share common ground with Medieval and many Renaissance works, where the preparation and resolution of dissonance only added shape by means of tension and relaxation to a musical architecture which was static owing to the absence of modulation. The nature of such musical processes was, of course, ideally suited to the new Expressionist aesthetic of the early twentieth century, dependent as it was on motionless dreamscapes which erupted from the confining walls of the subconscious. For no matter how frenetic or otherwise the apparent activity, the vision remains rooted, unable to escape from obsessional self-regarding.

A further contribution towards the static nature of the new music, and a most important factor in Schoenberg's attempts to find substitutes for the form-building propensity of tonality, is the use of material which is always stated at its original pitch, even when, as often happens, the rhythmic contours are varied. Variation by octave displacement is also employed, but this does not radically alter the effect of fixing a motive firmly in its place in the chromatic hierarchy as an unchanging point of reference for our ears to recognize. The fourth of the Five Orchestral Pieces makes some use of this technique of formal orientation, along with other methods, and something of its substance should be examined.

The same tight motivic organization exists in this piece as in the first of the set, governing both the material that develops and grows as well as that which conforms to the 'fixed-pitch' principle. However, our present interest lies in such figures as are marked in Ex. 14 from what

Ex. 14

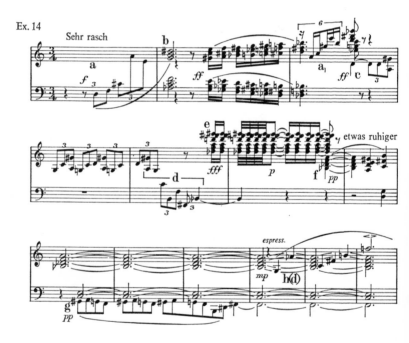

might be called the exposition, and in their recurrence at fixed pitch in Ex. 15, which gives a sizeable portion of the first thematic engagement. Unlike the body of the first movement, which showed a steady build-up, this section plunges after the exposition into a hectic development of virtually uniform interest and density. Motives are juggled and

(texture not always complete)

rhythmically distorted to yield new adjacencies and relationships. It is as if the steps in musical argument whereby the first piece reached its climax are here avoided, and the intensity of the process necessitates its speedy exhaustion. There follows a lull, and just as quickly a further thematic maelstrom builds up to cut the movement suddenly off. The implication of such a piece is that the state of 'becoming' which informs so much post-Renaissance music finds a substitute in the presentation of a single state or condition. The complex network of tensions which comprises a subconscious state has a history, but a piece like 'Peripetie' seems to be about that state rather than about the process in time which went to its making. Thus, a musical illusion is created of presenting in an instant of time the experience which previous ages had seen as an unfolding process: in place of the progress of feeling from one point in time to another, the music presents the experiential state of one who has just arrived after the same journey.

OTHER MIDDLE-PERIOD WORKS

The recurrence of material at fixed pitches is more obvious in *Das Buch der hängenden Gärten*. One should be careful not to see everything that Schoenberg did during his 'free' atonal period as a step towards serialism and twelve-note writing. But there is an obvious connexion between the harmonic and thematic deployment of a complex of notes which persistently returns and the continual revolutions of a series. The inventive ingenuity with which Schoenberg wrings ever varied effects from this single formal procedure is highly characteristic. The tenth song is typical in the way the piano part manipulates the material of the opening six bars (Ex. 16) throughout the rest of the song. Bars 7–12 amount to a variation, but one in which vertical and horizontal factors are already interacting: the seventh and eighth bars cut out the original melodic decoration, which now appears in the voice, while the next two take bars 3 and 4 of the exposition section, and fashion something entirely new by shifting the adjacencies so that passing notes now coincide with harmonies and harmonic notes become melodic (the G sharp on the first beat of bar 2, for instance, is isolated in bar 9). The tendency for harmonies to be melodically explained, or, perhaps, to prove that they were melodic in origin all along (arrived at by conflation) is further exemplified in bars 11 and 12 where the piano right hand

Ex. 16

unfolds a chromatic scale—with octave displacement—from A to F. This corresponds to the right hand of bars 5 and 6, except that the F was originally a harmony note. The rhythmic diminution of the same figure in the left hand demands more notes to fill the bar, and these include the remaining harmonies from bars 5 and 6. It is as if we are shown harmony on the point of evolving from melody (the logical outcome of increasingly close stretto entries is a homophonic chord progression). The last seven bars of the song provide a further juggling of previously heard elements at their original pitch, and the melodic decoration omitted in the first variation is now expanded. This obsessional reviewing of a limited set of motives is an ideal embodiment of the imprisoned thoughts of Expressionism—in the present case, the continued longing of desire unsatisfied after one short kiss.

29

Naturally, the broader aspects of form do not apply in a piece as short as this song, and the same can be said of many other pieces by Schoenberg at this time. Basically all large-scale forms derive from the need to maintain interest in the widest sense (this includes introducing enough new ideas to engage the attention, but not more than the mind can assimilate at once); and in a short piece of this nature limited material will not outlive its welcome nor will widely ranging material tax concentration. In fact, Schoenberg only solves the problem of how to construct the sentence. Interest is maintained by phrase manipulation in no particularly systematic way, though one can see growth on a tiny scale in the extensions of the chromatic scale idea. The first song, however, does show a formal approach of more widely applicable interest, in that several separate elements, exposed at the outset, come into collision during the course of the piece, and become more tightly bound to each other while for the most part retaining their original pitches. Ex. 17

Ex. 17

gives some of these elements and two of the subsequent events which bring them together. This process, closely allied to contrapuntal growth, is seen to work by opposite means in a short phrase from the first of the Three Piano Pieces opus 11. Bars 4 to 8 show a phrase built out of three little cells which grow in length through a loosening of the ties between them. What had seemed like a single entity becomes a thematic complex of jostling ideas. The constantly changing accents and phrase lengths, heard against the subconscious background of our expectations, produce contrapuntal growth of a sort. This method, normally seen as a further example of the composer's variation technique, has in fact, a more precise formal application. The irregular phrasing of the ostinato in the first of the Five Orchestral Pieces, for instance, produces the same effect, so that the piling on of parts as the movement progresses provides more than an increasing density; rather is there a growing counterpoint of accents heard and unheard.

Other structural methods are to be seen in what amounts to a summary of all Schoenberg's atonal findings, *Pierrot lunaire*. This again does not move much beyond the construction of sentence-like forms; once material has been exposed, and development of the sort already discussed has begun, there is rarely a need for more than one further crucial decision to be made, since a single formal 'happening' is all that is necessary to give shape. In the first movement, for instance, 'Mondestrunken', much of the music spins along on a constantly recurring figure—the ultimate point to which material of fixed pitch can lead—and in theory, the piece could have completed the course under its own momentum, like other movements in the work, or, indeed, like many items from *Das Buch der hängenden Gärten*, where a single

Ex. 18

statement or sentence is often all that is required. But there is a feeling of expectancy aroused by the tinkling ostinato that must be fulfilled, the tension accumulating from the unchanging oscillation round a few notes needs an outlet, and after a short sequential treatment of the ostinato, suggested by the whole-tone shape of the first three notes, Schoenberg launches a new texture, excitingly extending the formal horizon of the piece (Ex. 18). Even here, though, the musical form is dictated by the verse structure, since the placing of the climax corresponds to the last verse of the poem. In fact, many formal and textural details throughout stem from the formalism of the text, each poem consisting of two four-line sections followed by a five.

The feeling in 'Mondestrunken' of a change of emphasis in the music, an outcome or result, is the nearest we get to movement, though it is no more than the transition from one static plane to another. Of the single-process movements which once started do not need to change course, perhaps the most tightly closed and self-sufficient are canonic pieces like 'Parodie' and 'Mondfleck'. A sure way of establishing any material a composer cares to use is to repeat it—a universal musical principle of development or growth. Schoenberg's use of fixed-pitch material embodies this principle, although in the rhythmic variation and octave displacement to which such motives are subjected we can see his attempt to break free from the overt repetition (including sequence) of previous styles, using constant variation as a camouflage. In the canonic items from *Pierrot lunaire* there is possibly a rapprochement between the desire both to grow and vary continually and to establish melodic shapes by the strict repetition which canonic forms yield. Order is thus wrung from melodic anarchy, sanity from chaos. Nevertheless, 'Parodie' is still dependent on the verse structure, for each two-line section receives different canonic treatment on a new theme, except where exact verbal repetition brings back the original subject. The character of the various themes is dictated by considerations of word painting: the clicking of the knitting needles, the lovesick duenna, the whispering and giggling of the breeze, but the building principles are less tangible. Entry points, decision on whether to invert or not seem to rest on the avoidance of octave doubling, on the wish to saturate the texture with chromaticism, and on the needs of the composer's inner ear for a particular instrumental timbre and density of texture.

The following song, 'Mondfleck', one of the most quoted of all examples of twentieth-century counterpoint, seems even more to consist of a single expressive idea, shaped at one blow. The retrogression at the mid-point of the movement of the top two voices, which, proceeding at twice the pace of their canonic partners in the piano, need such a process to fill out their allotted bars, provides a single entity of tightly bound relationships each balancing the other in a perfectly tensed organism. Such a form, one feels, even more than in the omnipresent motive work of, say, the first of the Five Orchestral Pieces, justifies itself in every bar, so close are the ties between the related parts. Perhaps a structure which governs so much of the textural articulation of a movement allows too little room for the creative 'chance happening', is possibly too pre-compositionally determined, but the voice part gives some measure of freedom.

One type of movement which has not yet been touched upon, yet which is arguably the most obvious outcome of Expressionism's subconscious delving, is exemplified in the last of the Five Orchestral Pieces, the third of the Three Piano Pieces Opus 11, and 'Enthauptung' from *Pierrot lunaire*. Here one finds the freely associative connexions of subconscious logic in full play. Only by forcing the point can any of the formal procedures so far discussed be applied. The orchestral piece is the most ambitious of these three examples, and tells us a great deal about Schoenberg's mind and methods—illuminates for us, perhaps, many odd corners of his subsequent work on which little light is normally thrown. The writing here is unsystematic, and the piece seems to have been composed in an improvisatory way. It is no doubt interesting to see this and that referential point or stabilizing factor—the rhythmic articulation, for instance, of the endlessly proliferating but shapely tune, the recurrence of harmonic and textural motives (thirds, for instance, in the opening phrase)—but these cannot be viewed in the same light as the obviously conscious motive building in 'Nacht' and many another piece. It would be more realistic to suppose that Schoenberg composed it quite freely and naturally as an earlier master might have improvised an impromptu at the piano. The form of the piece is dictated by the rise and fall of its endless melody. Harmonies and textures were shaped in support as the fancy took him. Nothing is more characteristic of the composer than the elaboration one finds here, with the music ranging from five to eight parts and more. At several points it would in theory make little difference if the momentary thickening of the polyphony were excised. Such luxuriant details are however as typical of his intellectual exuberance as they were of Bach, and as they were untypical of, say, Handel. So much is going on here, and in many other highly complex movements, such as 'Mondfleck', that part of the expressive idea would seem to be to provide a symbol of something impossible to perceive direct. Such is the speed and density of Schoenberg's feeling in time, and so far beyond simple understanding are the complex patterns of subconscious experience he is attempting to shape in his art, that a symbol is required which we can never really recall in detail. Experience almost too bewildering for the human mind to encompass is given an appropriate representation.

The form in these more freely composed pieces seems dependent on a much simpler conception of counterpoint. The third of the Three Piano Pieces, for example, fills out its textures with wholesale chordal doubling, and the harmonic palette which Schoenberg allows himself here gives us a key to the vertical aspects of more contrapuntal scores which are systematic in their motive derivations, but do not so easily yield to harmonic analysis. These do no more than show Schoenberg's preferences for the sheer sound properties of certain combinations, and again one must guard against trying to find a systematized interaction of vertical and horizontal in works which do not grow strictly from previously stated premises. Conflation of melodic motives is to be found, as is fixed-pitch harmonic repetition, but more often than not this aspect of his music seems to be freely felt. The subtle flavour of this harmony lies in Schoenberg's method of placing chordal segments culled from tonality alongside his own synthetic aggregations in an almost bi-tonal way. The climactic Ex. 19 from *Erwartung* epitomizes Schoenberg's

Ex. 19

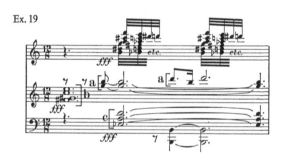

harmonic vocabulary, consisting as it does of triad (*a*), whole-tone element (*b*), and perfect fourth and augmented fourth (*c*), while giving the feeling of a dominant discord.

The acceptance of Schoenberg as a composer who could write in this free manner completes a picture of someone less restricted in method than analytical explanations of the more tangible aspects of his technique have led many to believe. In the works so far examined, techniques from the most elusive and improvisatory to the most tightly bound can be found in direct juxtaposition and also in combination in the same passage. The canons in 'Parodie', for instance, are accompanied by a rhythmically free piano part which has recourse to a fanciful elaboration and motivic exploration of its own. In between these extremes, we find varying shades of emphasis, including writing such as occurs in the first orchestral piece, where the speed of composition and unity of conception make it difficult to distinguish between conscious connexions and those which a composer of Schoenberg's intellect working under pressure of inspiration would produce intuitively.

The triumph of Schoenberg's less consciously systematic style is to be found in *Erwartung*, one of the most remarkable examples of sustained free composition in existence. It is perhaps the high-water mark of his pre-serial atonal period, and at the same time provides an emotional *ne plus ultra* which made some such system as twelve-note writing an absolute psychological necessity. Attempts have been made to analyse this score, but their restricted success seems merely to confirm the work as a giant improvisation, controlled by the drama of the text, which elicits a nervous, hallucinatory response of the most minute precision. A search for the referential features which orientate many atonal forms discovers only details of strictly local importance and application—the vertical aspects of the opening phrases, for instance, are coloured by aggregations of fourths, fifths, and tritones—although Alexander and Walter Goehr have shown an overall dramatic purpose and shape behind the vocal line. Otherwise, the piece is dictated by freely associative variation and development, and by the composer's reaction to the nightmare emotional life of the woman. Such unifying factors as we can find would be the natural result of an inspiration which unbelievably took the composer only eighteen days to set down.

The most astonishing aspect of the work is its rhythmic freedom, and the particular way musical tension and relaxation are deployed within the static framework typical of atonality. The disconnectedness of the woman's half-spoken thoughts, the excited spurts and sudden hesitancies find a response in mercurially contrasted fragments, and the pace and density changes sometimes from bar to bar, such is the speed of Schoenberg's musical thought. Phrases whose rhythm and harmonic tension seek a dynamic outlet are balanced by absolutely static paragraphs. These various facets of musical feeling in time cancel each other out and create a complex state of immobility.

The static and dynamic aspects of music might be considered the most important element of an art that exists in time, and in any work one of these two opposed musical concepts will be taken as the norm, the other related to it. Thus, the static variation movement in an essentially dynamic classical symphony will be seen as a momentary pause against a moving background. A work like *Erwartung*, however, neutralizes such dynamic properties as its phrases possess, since the complexity of rhythm and phrase never allows a recognizable pulse to be established. If later works in the twelve-note manner continue the atonal textures of *Erwartung*, it must be said that they mostly have a simpler rhythmic layout, and return to a dynamic, forward-moving norm. Perhaps the harmony is immobilized by the continual revolutions of the series, but in, for example, the Third and Fourth Quartets the rhythmic configuration returns to a classical concept of time—one of several characteristics which embody Schoenberg's transcendence of Expressionism.

It was suggested above that *Erwartung* was an embodiment of all that forced Schoenberg on to the road to twelve-note writing, and we might summarize here the position the composer now found himself in. Forms have grown shorter, owing to the compression and intensity of feeling characteristic of Expressionist ideals. Yet it cannot be doubted that much in the composer's nature wanted to expand. Early works like *Gurrelieder*, the First Quartet, and *Pelleas* support this, as does the intensity of the subsequent shorter pieces. It is noticeable, for instance, that this particular emotional pressure does not invade similar short essays by Webern, whose microcosmic world was more at one with itself. It might be thought that Schoenberg's problems had been solved in a work like *Erwartung*, a broad half-hour structure in his free atonal style. But this was not so. The work is really an isolated achievement, consisting of a chain of the sort of ideas and structures found in shorter pieces. They are unified by the text and by the fact that the expressive idea called for the presentation of a single soul state. It is the answer to a specific artistic problem which could not conceivably recur. Moreover, in order to sustain on this scale the sort of density of experience found in pieces a fraction of its length, Schoenberg must have become dangerously dependent on the wells of his subconscious activity. Further steps in the same direction would have led to a spiritual death. No personality can grow by feeding on itself, and a man of Schoenberg's aspiring nature and will to explore and renew himself would have been doubly conscious of the fact. Consequently, we can feel after the period of *Erwartung* and *Pierrot lunaire* a steady effort to expand the frontiers of his musical universe by freeing himself from the confines of personal feeling.

SERIALISM

The musical result of this urge was a change in the relationship between his creative consciousness and his musical language. Elements of harmony, rhythm, melody, and texture, products of Expressionism which had originally sprung from the subconscious, were forcibly taken and bent to a constructional will which was no longer imprisoned by personal psychology. In depersonalizing his material in this way, Schoenberg won a spiritual victory comparable to that of Beethoven in his last period, and significantly did so at the same time of life—for we tend to forget that Schoenberg did not produce a twelve-note work until he was fifty.

The first steps towards placing his material outside himself can be seen in works which exhibit in varying degrees increasingly systematic methods for ensuring that all twelve notes of the chromatic scale are kept in constant play, a natural development of the chromatic saturation and avoidance of octaves found in his previous work. There is also the use of motivic shapes (which we now call series) to integrate the harmonic and melodic aspects of his music, though not at first comprehensively. Again one can see in this latter tendency a logical extension of those procedures in pre-serial atonal works where melody can be seen emerging from harmony, and vice versa. Of deep significance to our understanding of Schoenberg is the fact that the works which embody these characteristics, *Die Jakobsleiter*, the Five Piano Pieces opus 23, and the Serenade opus 24, shows the beginnings of a more detached art, a less personally involved attitude to the music on the composer's part. More important, the first of these essays, *Die Jakobsleiter*, concerns itself with a spiritual problem which was to occupy the composer at various times for the rest of his life: 'learning how to pray', a process which requires complete submission of the ego. A book which was much in Schoenberg's mind at that time, Balzac's *Seraphita*, supplied the composer with much of the spiritual content of *Die Jakobsleiter*, and also, in its concept of Heaven, provided a striking literary analogy with what was to become Schoenberg's method of composing with twelve notes. One much-quoted passage runs as follows: 'Light gave birth to melody, and melody to light; colours were both light and melody; motion was numbered by the Word; in short, everything was at once sonorous, diaphanous, and mobile; so that, everything existing in everything else, extension knew no limits, and the angels could traverse it everywhere to the utmost depths of the infinite.' Schoenberg acknowledged his debt to this vision in an exposition of his theory of 'musical space', as embodied in twelve-note practice: 'In this space . . . there is no absolute down, no right or left, no forward or backward. Every musical configuration, every movement of tones has to be comprehended primarily as a mutual re ation of sound, of oscillatory vibrations, appearing at different places and times.' The extent to which Schoenberg's visionary statement is applicable to our aural experience of form and content in the twelve-note works will be discussed in due course. Meanwhile, we find in *Die Jakobsleiter* examples of total chromaticism and serialism which add up to a free twelve-note usage. This extends earlier motive-work without establishing an all-embracing principle. Ex. 20, from the

Ex. 20

very opening of the work, for example, exposes two hexachords which unfold the complete chromatic scale, reserving one for the harmonic accumulation, and the other for the ostinato figures. It will be noticed that the content of the six-note ostinato is frequently re-ordered, at first retaining the content of each two-note group, but later abandoning even that limitation, as the texture grows in complexity. The method is that of Hauer's so-called tropes, in which the twelve notes of the chromatic scale are divided into two hexachords, or groups of six notes. These are used as note quarries for harmony and melody, but are not ordered specifically within themselves.

The other aspect of Schoenberg's development at this time, his use of note series whose content is strictly ordered, appears tentatively in both the Serenade opus 24 and the Five Piano Pieces opus 23. However, his application of serial methods here suggests that he still had not seen the technique in a revelatory way, and it is a mistake, if we are to experience the excitement of Schoenberg's discoveries, to view twelve-note writing as the inevitable outcome of the language problems posed by music at that time. If language were the only factor involved, it is conceivable that the trope method used at the beginning of *Die Jakobsleiter*, or the mixture of free elements and non-twelve-note series found in the piano pieces, might have served him adequately. Certainly the serial working in opus 23 no. 4 is such that the four little and frequently cryptic series on which the piece is based can only have been seen as extensions of the referential and motivic techniques of his earlier music. In fact, although the new spirit of his music seemed to be leaving the Expressionist orbit, this transitional serialism still seems incapable of placing the notes in detached perspective.

Ex. 21, for instance, gives the exposition of the series in opus 23, no. 4,

Ex. 21

and Ex. 22 a subsequent use so garbled that Schoenberg still seems too close to his material, pulling it about to suit his personal whims. He still had to learn how to let it do a little of the work for him, just as, to draw an analogy, the classical composer could assume certain formal principles which he need not wilfully distort. The fact that twelve-note serial pieces (opus 23, no. 5, for instance) took their place beside equally valid but freer methods proves that he was still not sure of his destination.

So does his continued production of small forms in the style of his Expressionist period. He could hardly realize, perhaps, that he was on the point of transcending himself completely and finding an answer to the problems, both linguistic and aesthetic, of constructing large forms.

In fact, as is so often the case with the discovery of principles of universal significance, whether philosophical, religious, or artistic, understanding dawns by degrees over a period of time. We may take it that with the composition of the Suite opus 25, for piano solo, the composer's first work to use a single twelve-note series throughout, Schoenberg consolidated the discovery which had been staring him in the face for some time, but whose profound truth he had not at first fully appreciated. For, although it is easy to see in retrospect an orderly chain of development in opus 23's and opus 24's preliminary essays in serialism, the compositional principle embodied in the Suite marks a gigantic stride. If we view Schoenberg's problem purely in terms of language, the point loses its force. But related to psychological needs, the final step is seen to be of crucial importance. For in lighting upon a method whereby a single ordered pattern of twelve different notes would supply the material for a complete work, Schoenberg had gravitated from mere compositional techniques to a law, something which he could view as, in a sense, existing outside himself, and which his world of feeling could live by. This enabled Schoenberg, in the period directly following, to embark on a series of purely instrumental works of grand proportions, the Wind Quintet, the Suite opus 29, the Third Quartet, and the Variations for Orchestra.

The relationship of the twelve-note series to this achievement is, however, not straightforward. It has been said that the continual revolutions of a series finally supplied Schoenberg with a satisfactory substitute for the tonality whose absence he had been combating in various ways for the previous fifteen years. But this does not seem justified by the facts, for his earlier motive development could, in theory, have supported such structures. What it did do was to guarantee the relevance of every facet of the score and supply an endless chain of notes with which to continue. It thus released him from the freely associative and thereby completely 'self'-dependent method of generating each new move, where the placing of notes in time and space was too little limited by opening premises. If, as the facts suggest, it did not dictate larger formal processes, the new method did represent a petrifaction of the textural essence of his free atonal music, by integrating vertical and horizontal, and by guaranteeing total chromaticism and motivic relevance. As such, it enabled Schoenberg to distance himself from Expressionism. He now no longer need to limit his forms by the compression suited to Expressionism, and in the period of spiritual relaxation and calm which followed his emergence on the other side of his Expressionist experience he could afford to refer back uninhibitedly to classical formal precedents in working out his newly expansive concepts.

(This new-found freedom is pushed to its logical conclusion in the series of American works in which Schoenberg encompasses his beginning by returning to an apparently much simplified tonal language. But to call the Suite for strings, Variations for wind band, Variations on a Recitative for organ, and completed Second Chamber Symphony simply tonal would be to belie the subtlety of the rapprochment Schoenberg has achieved there. During the period of his break from orthodox tonality Schoenberg had not only eschewed its constructional properties but had avoided all references to the vocabulary of triadic and octave-based harmony. His return at this later period to the vocabulary does not presume a similar grammatical usage. The triadic chords we find here are governed by a logic which admits the experience of free association and serialism. In another of these works, *Kol Nidre*, for instance, we find tonal elements operated upon serially. As a corollary of this, Schoenberg now allowed himself tonal or triadic references within his strictly twelve-note pieces—the Piano Concerto is a prime example. But in neither of these two cases should individual elements be confused with the logic which dictates their behaviour.)

The works produced after his discovery of the twelve-note method are so rich in invention and textural possibilities that the scope of the technique appears inexhaustible. Schoenberg's skill in manipulating the forty-eight series to be gained from the eleven possible transpositions of a work's basic row attained to such phenomenal mastery that it could encompass styles ranging from the classical, embodying traditional melodic, contrapuntal, and rhythmic procedures, to something nearer the extraordinary processes of his free atonal period. Almost every work which uses a series uncovers some new method of tapping its resources. In most cases the series for a work was an abstraction consciously derived from an original melodic idea. This idea might have come immediately to the composer as a melody of twelve notes, or else the series might have been more consciously constructed to make it workable, that is to say, capable of the sort of manipulation which will be briefly exemplified below. (The formal ground plan of such a work might be said to be a factor outside the series, which is related to it only in that it should be able to supply the sort of melody and harmonic texture suited to fill out the structure as already conceived. See p. 51.)

SCHOENBERG'S TWELVE-NOTE TECHNIQUE

For a preliminary survey of Schoenberg's twelve-note technique his procedures may be divided into two main categories: those in which one form of the series at a time supplies every facet of the texture, and those in which two or more forms appear simultaneously. An examination of two passages from the Theme and Variations movement in the Suite opus 29 will show what factors dictate the successions of series in the former case, and will also give some hint of how Schoenberg derives thematic material from his row. First, the series itself should be examined. It possesses remarkable characteristics:

first the initial hexachord of *O*–E flat[1] finds its six notes retained, but re-ordered in those of *I*–B flat, *R*–F and *RI*–C (in many cases also keeping intact the note-group E flat–G–G flat–B flat) as well as in the transpositions of those four forms by a major third up and down (Ex. 23). This means, in effect, that on reaching the half-way point in

Ex. 23

any row Schoenberg can move by analogy to any of eleven other forms, and complete a twelve-note series while availing himself of variations in the note order. Likewise, any one of those forms can follow any other without a single note being repeated in adjacent hexachords. This develops the principle that all twelve notes should be exposed before any one of them is repeated, although there are many ways of rationalizing a relaxation of this rule. Again, the series begins and ends with a major third. This means that at the end of any one serial statement, there are immediately *O*, *R*, *I*, and *RI* forms available beginning with the last two notes stated. In this way, chains of series can be formed (Ex. 24).

The accompaniment to the main theme of the movement is entirely dependent on this latter process. Firstly, it uses each of the four basic forms: *O* and *R*, which have the D flat–F segment in common, and then, using the E flat 'tonic' or 'final' of the series as a pivot, the *I* and *RI* forms, linked by the same segment. But this is only as it first appears.

[1] The abbreviations *O*, *I*, *R*, and *RI* will be used to denote the row forms, Original, Inversion, Retrograde, and Retrograde Inversion, and they are followed by the degree of the scale on which the row starts, or, as far as retrograde forms are concerned, ends.

The order of the notes F sharp and A in the fourth bar could be accepted as a reshuffling for the sake of a passing preference, but, in fact, Schoenberg has availed himself of the variation of *RI*–E flat's hexachord obtained in *I–F*. Similarly in bar 6, the order F–A flat tells us that *R–B*'s first hexachord has been used to vary *O–A*'s. Subsequent series progress without complication using *O* and *RI* forms alternately by means of the major third segment, so that a sequential chain is constructed, each link lying a tone lower than the last.

Of greater interest is the theme itself, a folk-song, 'Aennchen von Tharen', in simplest E major, whose incorporation into the textural scheme will begin to suggest how material of virtually any kind can be extracted from a twelve-note series (Ex. 24). This kind of manipulation, incidentally, is of great help in obtaining new linear shapes from a row which is more harmonic than melodic in its layout. There are, for instance, five major thirds, two minor thirds and four semitones, which, accounting for inversions gained from octave transpositions, means that only six of the available eleven intervals within an octave are used, and a hearing of the work suggests that the sound of harmonic textures in thirds and sixths was uppermost in the composer's mind when constructing his series. Ex. 25, taken from the second variation, shows Schoenberg more obviously availing himself of the hexachordal

Ex. 25

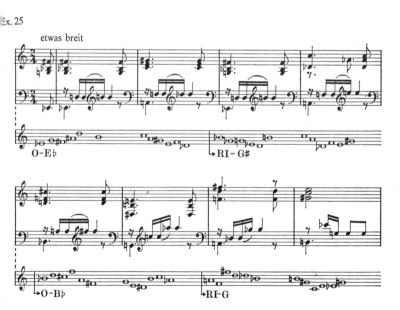

re-ordering to be obtained within the twelve-set complexes of which Ex. 23 was an example. Notice that the conflation of the first four notes into chords in each case disguises the order, so that it is not until the fourth bar that one realizes a different row has been substituted. A similar method is used in the next four-bar phase, but this time the substitute row yields a more drastic re-ordering as befits a later stage in the melodic argument. A final point of interest is that the choice of O–B flat in the fifth bar is dictated by the tune (seen in the piano's left-hand cross-over part). Having been serially integrated at the outset, this tune can now be allowed to suggest procedures, and as its second phrase sets out a fifth higher, a serial transposition of a fifth accompanies it.

To move on to the second category of serial usages, one method whereby different rows can be used simultaneously is inferable from a procedure described above. If any of the forms in Ex. 23 were combined with a retrograde version of any of the other eleven, it follows that the initial hexachords would present all twelve notes, and the same applies, naturally, to the second hexachords. It can be stated fairly generally, in fact, that two series will be combined when this property obtains, and an interesting extension of the principle is often found in later twelve-note works by Schoenberg, where series are so constructed that the inversion at a fifth below produces this relationship with the original. The row of the Violin Concerto is an example (Ex. 26), and once again it seems that tonal habits die hard.

Ex. 26

Rows are combined in this way when the composer wants to make use of their melodic properties against a fairly simple texture, for obviously the production of a whole texture from one row necessitates a denial of its linear character. A few bars from the opening of the Violin Concerto provide a perfect example of this method (Ex. 27). The whole of this section is a locus classicus of inspired serial economy, for the two series quoted in Ex. 26 plus their retrogrades provide all the music up to bar 47. The use to which these series are put in the first tutti is especially instructive. The density of musical interest here involves

Ex. 27 poco allegro

four textural layers and produces a combination of the methods just described, *O*–A governing the top two parts and *I*–D the lower. A single row here would have been unmanageable; with two, the composer can take up twice the length with each rotation of his series and control more successfully the melodic aspect of the texture (Ex. 28). The means whereby the chords in the bass are built from *I*–D are discussed below.

The use of a single row can, of course, be countenanced in a dense texture of merely harmonic interest, and a few bars earlier we see how Schoenberg can increase harmonic intensity in preparation for his climax, while also giving an example of the sort of licence he allowed himself with note-orders. It can be seen that the first two notes of each hexachord are split away from the main body of the row, and lead an existence independent of the remaining notes which supply harmony (Ex. 29). The way was prepared for this process, when, in the opening bars, the same division of notes between tune and accompaniment was presented without upsetting the strict note-order. This is a further example of the new role given to motives already justified by strict usage (compare the folk-tune in Ex. 24), but it also embodies a far

subtler process. The slow rotation in the solo part of four of the row's notes means that the increase in rhythmic interest in the accompaniment is steadied by the rotation of only eight notes. This control of harmonic tension places weight on the tutti when it bursts out with all twelve notes in immediate play.

A variation of the method by which hexachordally related rows are combined is obtained by splitting the row into smaller segments of three or four notes each, and then using in counterpoint or accompaniment whichever segments are not being employed in the main statement. The opening of the Fourth Quartet and Ex. 28 exemplify this, and in the second of the Six Choruses opus 35 we also see it deployed with great resource—using repetitions which relate logically to the procedure shown in Ex. 29—and with the same intention of harmonic control in a quick rhythm (Ex. 30). The row is seen complete in the top part. The ramifications and logical extensions of the one or two procedures and methods set out above are endless, and most of Schoenberg's textural engineering and serial ingenuities can be related to them, for the broad principles which govern this aspect of his composition remained largely the same to the end of his life.

This account of the composer's adaption of a twelve-note row to his general textural requirements should be complemented with instances of its application to the more specific problems posed by medium, a neglected aspect of the technique which confirms its eminent practic-

ability, in the hands of Schoenberg at least. The specialized nature of the writing needed for a work like the Six Choruses for male voices, facing as it does a restricted vocal range and the consequent danger of monotony, gives us a most valuable insight into this side of the composer's technique. The passage quoted above (Ex. 30) shows a characteristic result. In order to maintain some kind of linear independence and coherent part-writing within the restricted range, the lines have to eschew the larger vocal intervals. The way the series is used stems almost entirely from this textural consideration, for in order to maintain vitality in the face of this melodic limitation, Schoenberg repeats the little three-note motives. The more leisurely course of the top line provides contrast, and also compels several repetitions of each accompanying group in order to avoid octaves and keep all twelve notes in play. An added practical consideration is that these repetitions make the choir's task a little easier. The whole movement can be seen as a perfect integration of practical musicianship and compositional technique within a serial orbit. The same restrictions apply in the fifth movement, where the density of the textural conception frequently requires that the chorus be split into eight parts. The thematic working depends on a series of ostinatos often doubled at the rhythmic unison

to produce writing which constantly varies a collection of two-note figures (Ex. 31). A special kind of malleability is required of the series here, and its inversion at the fifth below can be seen not only to re-order *O* hexachordally in the approved manner but to retain each two-note group (Ex. 32). This gives immediate variation possibilities and focuses the complex texture by emphasizing the same two-note groups, a method which takes account of the simpler, bolder writing needed if such density of choral layout is to remain articulate.

Ex. 32

It is interesting from the same point of view to see what happens in the initial variation of opus 31. This was Schoenberg's first large-scale orchestral work to use a twelve-note row, and followed a series of chamber pieces where the method had yielded counterpoint of the purest kind. In order to meet the textural needs of a work for full orchestra, some of the thematic writing is doubled in thirds—a sonorous not a contrapuntal idea. This is serially justified by the fact that identical row forms a third apart yield an important correspondence. The row table in Ex. 33 shows that notes 1 and 2 and 8 and 9 (marked *x*) in the two rows in question produce an identical four-note nucleus, an intimate relationship which binds the rows together when they are stated simultaneously.

Ex. 33

Just as, earlier, the prospective analyst was warned that not too much was predictable from the 'information' given out during the expositions of Schoenberg's free atonal pieces, so now it must be said that the series of a work gives us only limited data bearing on possible motives, possible harmonies, and possible combinations of the two. The placing of these elements in space (texture) and time (rhythm) depends on the same compositional techniques for which we search the works of older masters. From this it will be deduced that form is also independent of the purely serial aspects of a work. In so far as tonality provided an incontrovertible means for integrating vertical and horizontal aspects of texture, there is a shared function with serialism, but its articulation of form through key finds other substitutes in Schoenberg's twelve-note work. In fact, it is by an increased activity and subtlety in other parameters of musical interest that Schoenberg achieves the variations and developments of traditional formal patterns found in his twelve-note works—by means of an interplay between varying levels of interest and intensity in the fields of melody, rhythm, and chromatic saturation (the part played by serialism in the latter two instances has already been hinted at in Ex. 29).

The opening of the Variations for orchestra provides an excellent example of the play between chromaticism and rhythmic articulation. Schoenberg's problem is to provide an introduction to the complete work and also to his initial statement of the main theme, which is a leisurely, long-breathed melody over static harmonies. Contrast must be provided, otherwise nearly sixty bars would pass before a dynamic element enters the work, and this is achieved by the steady rate of the quaver movement. But an equally lively rotation of the twelve chromatic notes would plunge us too quickly into the middle of things. The result would be fussy when the work as a whole is grand and spacious, and it would overshadow the theme's presentation. Instead, the row is unfolded gradually, and the chromatic density increases in a leisurely way, as notes are slowly added to the ostinato phrases (Ex. 34).

Ex. 34

The problems posed in the same field by larger formal considerations find masterly solutions in the Third Quartet, a work whose perfection of expression and design makes it a worthy successor to the late Haydn and middle-period Beethoven quartets. The first movement is a dynamic sonata form which works its passage against an ever-present quaver ostinato. At the outset, Schoenberg creates a type of motion by serial manipulation for which there are several classical precedents. He combines the forward-moving energy of his five-note ostinato in a brisk tempo with great breadth of feeling in the space taken to unfold the complete series (Ex. 35); compare the slow harmonic rhythm and quick pulse-rate of, say, the opening of Beethoven's First Razumovsky quartet. An increasing tension is maintained as the second subject approaches, by a steady growth and interaction of the lyrical parts of the texture, in which the ostinato also partakes, until the melodic activity

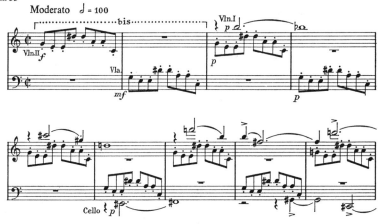

Ex. 35

begins to match the pace of the pattering quavers. Ex. 35 shows the ostinato and the first steps in the melodic argument, as question and answer alternate and then overlap. As energy accumulates, the ostinato can afford to free-wheel, and, influenced by the lyrical growth, proceeds for a while in tied quaver pairs and with imitative entries. Suddenly, at the point of maximum energy and density (triple-stopped chords have just been introduced) a new syncopation in the ostinato brakes the music hard down for the second subject, which employs the lapping paired quavers throughout its length. The speed of the chromatic rotation now equals the crotchet beat, and further growth is achieved in the irregular phrase-lengths—5 beats followed by 9 and 14 (8+6)—which contradict our expectations quasi-contrapuntally (in the manner familiar to us from Ex. 13). The development, charged with fresh energy by the dropping of two quavers from the ostinato, maintains impetus by means of phrase-length and rhythm, constantly remodelling the ostinato pattern and introducing a new sonorous element with double-stopped and open-string pizzicatos. A climax is reached, in which every bar is created out of one serial revolution. It is then subtly dissipated as the opening semitonal motive returns, without outward change of pace, in counterpoint which requires a bar and a half for each twelve-note set.

A further feature might be isolated to show Schoenberg's reflection of traditional processes: the coda builds tension only to be cut off on a half close (Ex. 36a); this hiatus is subtly prolonged by a triplet motion that keeps the imminent ostinato temporarily at bay, and the section

Ex. 36a

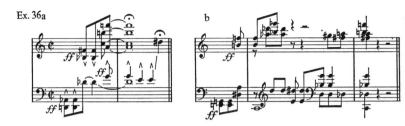

then closes with finality on an extension of the interrupted cadence (two twelve-note revolutions as against the earlier one, in an identical seven beats—Ex. 36a and b).

Whereas this movement is based on a steady quaver movement, against which variations of intensity contribute to a confident dynamism, its counterpart in the Fourth Quartet experiences more difficulty in its progress. The earlier work showed growth from a modest opening, and thus consolidated rhythmic ground incapable of disruption, but the present work opens with an almost too aggressive strength. Its bold top line and fierce accompaniment are almost immediately checked by the wry second phrase, whose inability to match top line and accompaniment denies a smooth passage to the repeat of the opening (Ex. 37).

Ex. 37   Allegro molto, energico

Rhythms jostle each other until the music's frustrated aim to propel itself forward bursts out into energetic triplets. Not surprisingly, the music runs out of energy before the second subject, withdrawing for a moment into a cloud of harmonics. The expressive quality of the section as a whole can be said to rest in a complex juxtaposition of simple forward motion with elements which seek to arrest the flow with a grinding of rhythmic gears.

The overt thematicism of these two quartets, and indeed of most of Schoenberg's twelve-note works, and the harmonic control described above, do allow traditional forms to influence his structures, but the vestiges of sonata, rondo, and other processes are subordinate to the composer's all-pervading principle of continual variation. In the first movement of the Fourth Quartet, for instance, one can trace a surface resemblance to sonata or perhaps sonata rondo form, but at the same time appreciate Schoenberg's claim to have freed himself from traditional patterns. The first ninety-five bars have a clear feeling of sonata exposition. The section has already been viewed up to the presentation of the second subject, and now it closes with a more determined rhythmic engagement after the traditional easing of tension for that passage. Thus it continues to reflect parallel sections in its sonata forebears. After a long section, developmental in feeling, which opens with the inverted main subject and includes a distinctive new theme, the main material is restated in condensed form at new pitches. A second development sequence of even greater intensity follows, before the coda caps the work with a further concentration of the principal themes—both subjects represented by their opening phrases. This ground plan is firmly signposted by uncomplicated thematic statements, but it is belied by a feeling of continuous growth and development which is typical of Schoenberg's unrelenting temperament. These statements take up very little room, and for the rest of the time he continually devises new shapes and textures. Their evolution from the series ensures their motivic relevance and the rhythm guarantees a more audible unity, but the impression is of continual extension. It would certainly have been possible in theory to make the interludes more dependent thematically on the exposition, rather than solely on the series itself, but Schoenberg's temperament was always opposed to the obvious. If motivic relevance was guaranteed, why overemphasize by thematic reference as well? It could also be said that the sharing of an identical source by all material, whether subsidiary or otherwise, demands the production of strong new ideas if monotony is to be avoided. This is of special importance in the development of a quasi-sonata structure like that of the Fourth Quartet's opening movement, when the exposition itself has been in a sense developmental.

The crucial point about such a movement, however, is that despite the sonata matrix discernible beneath the surface, Schoenberg could not enjoy the respite which the return of a home tonic undoubtedly afforded earlier composers. Thematic recurrence allows the movement to confirm its purpose by relating developmental stages to opening premises, but there is no emotional return, only a continual pioneering of new territory. This places as much weight on Schoenberg's powers of invention as did freer pre-twelve-note forms. And except that his subconscious did not have such influence on the music, the train of associative continuation which informed earlier pieces still played a powerful role in dictating thematic, textural, and rhythmic procedures against the twelve-note background.

Since all the stages in a movement (indeed in a work) have a common serial origin, rhythm becomes all-important in the derivation of new thematic material and new textures. From this point of view it is instructive to compare the opening movement of the Violin Concerto with that of the Fourth Quartet. For reasons which have already been formulated, Schoenberg uses new material in the 'vivace' central section, but whereas the first of such episodes in the quartet achieves a strong forward impulse through the rhythmic layout of the texture, the equivalent episode in the Concerto sounds static and freely episodic. It falls into four sections, loosely strung together, in which a propulsive dance strain alternates with a less strongly characterized background to the soloist's decorative display. The fact that the later stretches of the opening section were also fragmentary and decorative places great weight on the so-called return. It has to counterbalance some 100 bars of virtually non-developing material (again one speaks here in terms of rhythm and theme, not of serial motive), and the thematic compression, realignment, and extension make this passage the high point of the movement (bar 162). Although both these movements, like all twelve-note structures, are in effect series of variations, and are grounded on continuously evolving shape, they are nevertheless utterly different in expressive form. This has been very largely achieved by rhythm, and through the exploitation by that means of old associations. The first tutti in the concerto, for instance, sounds obviously ritornello-like (Ex. 28), yet never returns in that guise, while the continuous chain of new ideas for 161 of the movement's 265 bars is eased for the listener by the allusion to the exposition and central section of the traditional concerto. The looser formal contours, and the opportunities they create for accommodating display elements, mark a further traditional reference, and contrast strongly with the dynamic continuity of the quartet movement. In so far as such large-scale processes can be illustrated, Exx. 38 and 39 from the Quartet and Concerto respectively

Ex. 38

Ex. 39

show the rhythmic and textural manner by which Schoenberg attains his different ends.

In a movement like the 'Commodo' of the Fourth Quartet, the teeming invention which produces ceaseless variation and development is seen at its height. The minuet and trio form, with which it could conceivably be compared, is not signposted in the way the previous sonata is, and the material, often varied beyond recognition, is also shared between all main and subsidiary sections. The result sounds more like freely evolving pre-twelve-note forms, in spite of the squarer phrases and more conventional layout.

The method of formal continuation by inventing ever new and strongly characterized ideas leads inevitably to the single span of the Piano Concerto. Here, however, the skeleton of four traditional movements helps to explain for us the apparently endless sequence of new thought. In order to establish a stable point of departure for the amount of ground which is shortly to be covered, the opening movement dwells to a considerable extent on a single melody. The increasingly rich figurations which decorate its long and shapely lyricism, and the changes of pitch which operate within its characteristic rhythm (*cf.* Ex. 40) give the movement the air of a set of static variations. Yet a

Ex. 40

sonata form is also discernible: the repetition of the opening melody a fifth higher with a new contrapuntal motive in the piano sounds like the second group of a monothematic sonata, while the short central episode, although introducing new material which will be of prime importance in later movements, also works previously heard motives (*cf.* the less thematic development sections dealt with above). A truncated reference to the main tune is all that is needed for the return. From then on Schoenberg can afford to develop his argument at much greater speed, and it is not until the end of the finale that he pauses to consolidate ground with references back to previous movements.

It is unrealistic to regret the loss in the rhythmic simplifications which mark Schoenberg's classical twelve-note period of the extra-ordinary complexity of Expressionism, but there is no denying the fascination of its rediscovery in the String Trio. Just as the spiritual ground won by the twelve-note law had enabled links to be forged with pre-atonal forms, so now in old age Schoenberg could combine the

Ex. 41

seemingly irrational paragraphing of Expressionism with serial detachment. The mosaic juxtaposition of tiny sections which move forward with those that remain immobile, in a perfectly judged mesh of interlocking tensions, comprises the composer's crowning formal achievement (Ex. 41). Such elements of development and recapitulation as exist in the work's five continuous sections are obscured by the rhythmic complexity of the form and by the production of new material late in the work. One can perhaps also see there an extremely compressed form of the free evolution of sections found in parts of the concertos and the Fourth Quartet. Once again in Schoenberg's composing career can be felt the power of concentrated thought and feeling, but the subconscious urges of Expressionism are now replaced by the need to encompass the total experience of a lifetime. It is perhaps significant that another work written at this time, *A Survivor from Warsaw*, also forges links with the composer's Expressionist period, though in an overtly emotional way which the String Trio avoids. Formally it uses the same tiny motive cells as his pre-serial atonal works, and even though these are controlled by twelve-note procedures one feels that, as in the earlier period, the dramatic progression of the text is a crucial prop to the musical form. The String Trio's special achievement is that it brings about an even greater interpenetration of old and new in Schoenberg. Serialism is again aligned with something like an Expressionist compression in the rapid textural contrasts, but the radical juxtaposition of sentences and paragraphs finds no formal aid in text or drama. Again the squarer rhythms of his classical twelve-note period are often to be found in those paragraphs, yet the twelve-note usage itself moves beyond the idea of 'one series one law'. In fact the work is based on four six-note series from which several twelve-note rows can be constructed, and at a late stage it evolves a further series through a musically explained permutation (bar 184).

Except for the fact that for much of his career Schoenberg's multifarious achievements have avoided a strictly evolutionary development, we should be tempted to see the String Trio as the goal towards which all his previous works had striven. If the composer had lived to create more than the handful of works which followed it, its methods might have led to unexpectedly free extensions of his former strict twelve-note writing. As it is his later compositions already strike a resounding blow against those who see his music as a vehicle for the development of musical history. His work, like that of all great composers, constantly refers back as it presses forward, and it does so in an unpredictable way.